MAKING SERVICE
COUNT

How to Deliver Outstanding Customer Service
And Make Your Small Business More Profitable

TOM BORG

www.inkwaterpress.com

ISBN 1-59299-048-7

Publisher: Inkwater Press

Printed in the U.S.A.

DEDICATION

To all the of the hard working people who really care about their customers and do their best to make the time they spend with them a most pleasant and fulfilling experience.

To Colleen
More good days
are headed
your way
Sincerely
Tom Borg

ABOUT THE AUTHOR

Tom Borg is a consultant, trainer and author based in Canton, Michigan USA. His business articles have been published in over 46 countries. He is also the author of the book entitled Natural Prescriptions for the Good Life-A Fun and easy approach to make your life a continually growing and an invigorating experience.

You can reach him at:

Tom Borg
6426 Kings Mill Ct.
Canton, MI 48187
USA

(734)-453-8019
tomborg@comcast.net

TABLE OF CONTENTS

FOREWORD

The value of any business in the twenty first century will be directly measured by its customer service. Whether it be manufacturing, service or retail, customer service is the only criteria that will parallel the bottom line. Dr. Deming, the father of Japanese management, had this concept when he first introduced us to his "14 points" back in the 1940's.

In this book, MAKING SERVICE COUNT, Tom Borg has given us some solid tips for customer satisfaction which is the foundation that will benefit and improve every business that implements these ideas.

Over the past few years I have learned many techniques from Mr. Borg that have improved my business. My employees have benefited from his customer service programs. With his help and encouragement our company has risen to new levels of achievement; levels we could not have reached without his assistance.

Any information you glean from this book can assist you and your company in reaching its' service goals.

Successfully,
Richard Asztalos
President
Charisma Inc.
Laurel Park Place
Livonia, Michigan

INTRODUCTION

Small businesses all over the country are in the best position they have ever been in. It's no secret that the Fortune 500 companies have added no new jobs over the last 10 years. Because of the excess layers of management built up over the years and tougher competition, these companies have been forced to reduce the number of their employees. That's where small business has stepped in and created new job opportunities for Americans everywhere. While the work force of larger companies is shrinking, smaller companies are multiplying and dramatically increasing the number of their employees.

Congratulations for investing your money and time in reading this book. You will find the short, thought-provoking chapters are designed to help you to take action now!

When you answer the questions, do the exercises, and apply the principles and ideas covered in this learning tool, your customers' satisfaction level will go up and so will your profits.

This book is not meant to be a substitute for active participation in customer service education and development programs, but an additional resource. By implementing the practical ideas found in the chapters ahead you will be positioning your small business for success.

— Tom Borg

"It is one
of the most beautiful
compensations of this life
that no man can sincerely try to
help another without helping
himself."

— Ralph Waldo Emerson

TIP #1
BE A FRIEND!

One of the biggest advantages a small business person has is his ability to be a friend to his customers, to help them in a personable way to solve their problems. By setting the example for your staff or co-employees to follow, you are creating an opportunity for them to do a better job of serving customers.

Theodore Levitt, one of the national experts on customer service, says that "our customers want to have a business relationship with the people they buy from." Our customers want to feel special. They want to know that they are not just another number or some vague entity. Being in a small business, you have a golden opportunity to distinguish your company from the rest of the competition by being a friend.

There is a man from my hometown by the name of Joe Slaga, owner of PJ's, a baseball card shop. When customers enter his store, he makes them feel comfortable by his easy manner. He is a good people person. He realizes that people don't want to be badgered into buying anything. By joking and exchanging stories with them about their favorite sports celebrity, he develops a friendly relationship with all the adults and children who come into the store. He has made it a favorite stopping place for many children to bring their parents to browse and buy.

There are other baseball card shops in the area, but his is the busiest. How does he do it? Simple. He makes it a point to be a friend to his customers.

What are some of the things you, your staff and co-workers can do in your small business to be a friend to your customers? Hold a brainstorming session and make a list of seven ideas. Circle the top three ideas and take steps for implementing them this week.

ACTION PLAN:

7 things my staff and I can do to be more friendly with our customers:

1.

2.

3.

4.

5.

6.

7.

The 3 best ideas are:
Idea #1:

Person responsible to see that it is implemented:
The date it will be implemented:
Idea #2:

Person responsible to see that it is implemented:
The date it will be implemented:
Idea #3:

Person responsible to see that it is implemented:
The date it will be implemented:

"Remember that happiness is a way of travel - not a destination."

— Roy M. Goodman

TIP #2
YOUR ATTITUDE TOWARDS YOUR CUSTOMERS CAN MAKE THE DIFFERENCE

A few months back, a business owner approached me after one of my presentations and complained that he had been in the office supply business for over 20 years, during which time he had never seen it so bad as now. Customers were constantly trying to "nickel and dime him to death" on his prices. A local wholesale warehouse was selling many of the same items he carried at prices he couldn't touch. Customers were inconsiderate, rude, and impatient. He told me that in order to cope with this type of environment, he had started bluntly telling his customers that if they didn't like his prices or his service, they could take their business elsewhere. Needless to say, his business was doing poorly.

A few weeks later, I spoke to another office supply owner who was a competitor of the one above. I asked him how his business was doing. He smiled and told me his business had never been better. As he talked, he described how his customers were pleasant and good-natured and seemed to like coming in to his store. He told me that he treated many of them like they were part of his family. He felt his business was good because of his attitude towards life.

In these two examples, it's easy to see how the business owner's perspective shaped the amount of success he experienced with his business. When it comes to an attitude towards its customers, some businesses subscribe to Theory X. This theory states that customers are sneaky, troublesome, and motivated by narrow interests. Other businesses subscribe to Theory Y. This theory states that customers are fair and trustworthy people.

Paul Hawken, author of Growing a Business, says that 'being in business is not just about making money, but it is a way to become who you are." It makes good sense that if we are going to have a healthy business, we've got to start with a correct attitude towards ourselves as well as towards our customers.

Bob Tomsic, owner of a business machine repair company in Ann Arbor, Michigan, believes that one of the main reasons for his success is his intention of keeping all of his customers happy. He maintains that he has three sets of customers:

1) his family, 2) his employees, and 3) the people that need his company's services. By keeping all three groups satisfied, he has built a prosperous and growing company. This is not to say that there are not challenges in keeping these three sets of customers satisfied — there are. It's just that he understands that it is his philosophy towards these customers that makes the difference.

The interesting idea to note is that, despite the way we look at our business, it is up to us to "choose" the attitude we want to express. It's safe to say that the response we receive from our customers and employees or co-workers will be a reflection of the way we treat them.

As you look around your business community, you will see positive and negative examples of the viewpoint business owners display towards their customers. Note the ones who take a positive position, and make it a point to invest some time discussing successful business strategies with them. It will be worth it.

ACTION PLAN:

1. Three other business owners, managers or service employees in my community who have an
affirmative attitude towards their customers are:

-

-

-

2. Contact one of these people and set up a time
to have a cup of coffee and exchange effective
strategies.

3. My attitude towards my customers is:
       1 2 3 4 5 6 7 8 9 10
       poor   fair   good   excellent

4. Three things that can be done to improve my
attitude towards my customers:

-

-

-

5. Three long-range ideas to improve my employees' attitude towards the customer:

-

-

-

"Good manners
are but the visible parts
of unseen virtue."

— Anonymous

TIP #3
GREET AND ACKNOWLEDGE ALL CUSTOMERS ENTERING OR LEAVING YOUR STORE OR BUSINESS

There's a man by the name of Tony Grech who owns and runs Greko Printing & Imaging. Tony's print shop is one of the busiest in the area. Whenever I walk into his store, he calls me by name as he greets me. At first, I thought I was someone he particularly liked. We had discovered we were of the same nationality, Maltese, and his last name was the same as my uncle's. However, I soon discovered that he was genuinely friendly with all of his customers. He knows the majority of them by name, and if he doesn't know a person's name, he finds out immediately by asking. Many times there is a line of people waiting to speak with Tony or one of his assistants. It doesn't matter how long the line is, because as soon as that door opens and a customer walks in, he or she is acknowledged. If it will be a couple of minutes before Tony can get to the customer, he lets the person know. He thanks each one for understanding. The people wait patiently, because they know they will get the same personable attention. When a customer leaves, he or she is also given a cheerful goodbye.

What Tony and his staff are doing is helping their customers feel important. They want their customers to feel like they are somebody special. And as Tony says, "They are somebody special; they are my customers."

SELF QUIZ:

Circle the answers that apply to your business:

1. How do you, your staff or co-employees now acknowledge the customers that walk through the doors of your business?
   a. They are visually acknowledged within the first 10 seconds.
   b. They are given a verbal greeting within the first 10 seconds.
   c. They are asked an open-ended question pertaining to our services or products.
   d. They are ignored until they approach an employee with a question or want to pay for something.
   e. Sometimes we acknowledge them and sometimes we don't. It depends on how busy we are.

2. What are some of your ideas on how acknowledging customers can be done better? More consistently?

"Remember that a person's name is to that person the sweetest and most important sound in any language."

— Dale Carnegie

TIP #4
NAMES ARE IMPORTANT

Do you know the names of most of your customers? As Dale Carnegie said, "A person's name is to that person the sweetest, most important sound in any language." Research has shown that there is a particular chemical reaction that takes place in our brains when we hear our name.

An easy way to experiment with this idea is to walk into a crowded mall and call out in a loud voice a common name like Bob or Linda. You'll see many people by the name of Bob or Linda turn around and look at you.

If you or your employees are not regularly using the names of your customers, you are missing out on a technique that can help build a lasting relationship with them. An easy way to get and use the customer's name, if you don't remember it, is to read it off his check, credit card, or ticket stub. When in doubt, simply ask. A simple way to do this is to use the fill-in-the-blank method. It would work like this: "Hello, my name is Tom Borg, and your name is .....?

Once you get that person's name, use it in the conversation a few times. It helps to write down the names of the customers you have trouble remembering. Review the list from time to time. You'll be surprised and delighted at how easy you will be able to build a sincere rapport with your customers.

1. Name ten customers who frequent your business:

a.	f.
b.	g.
c.	h.
d.	i.
e.	j.

2. At your next meeting, hold a contest to see which one of your employees remembers the names of the most customers. Present him or her with a cash award.

3. Make it a point to run this contest from time to time at your employee meetings, making it clear that it is important to remember and use the name of the customers that do business with your company.

4. Look for ways to reward your employees between meetings when they remember and use their customers' names.

"The difference between ordinary and extraordinary is that little extra."

— Anonymous

TIP #5
LITTLE THINGS MAKE
A BIG DIFFERENCE:
1+1+2=112

As two business partners are being seated in a restaurant, they mention to the greeter that they are in a hurry. A few moments later, a waitress is ready to take their order. She acknowledges that they are on a tight schedule and will put a rush order on having their lunch prepared. A few minutes later, the waitress returns with the lunches and the bill. She suggests to the two men that if they would prefer to pay for their meal now, it would save them a few extra minutes when they are ready to leave. The two business partners agree and express their appreciation for her thoughtfulness.

So often, small business owners overlook the little things that mean so much to their customers. Running a business is like running a marathon; yet, some people run it like it was a 50 yard dash. They are in such a hurry to get to the finish line that the customer's real needs and wants are overlooked. Successful business owners realize that they are running a race, and this race is 26 miles and 385 yards long. They know that in order to be a winner, they must take care of the "little things" throughout the entire race. Like the old saying goes, "Being successful should never be confused with remaining successful." Successful business owners realize that they are in business for the long haul, not just the short ride. Take note of all the little things that are important to your customers. Set up a system to make sure these expectations are met. Remember, by taking care of the little things for your customers, it will help you earn their loyalty for life.

Three things that may be minor but do make a difference when we serve our customers are:

1.

Why is it important?

2.

Why is it important?

3.

Why is it important?

4. How are we going to implement these things into our business?

"Make it your business
to be happy and you are bound
to be happy in your business."

— Anonymous

TIP #6
MAKE IT FUN FOR YOUR CUSTOMERS TO DO BUSINESS WITH YOU

People like to have fun. They like to be able to enjoy themselves. One of the best opportunities for pleasure can occur when they do business with your company or organization.

Laughter is one of the few languages that is spoken by every human being. When your customers are met by cheerful, personable, and positive employees, chances are those customers will enjoy spending their money and do even more business with you.

Let's examine the psychology behind that kind of thinking. One of the main reasons why customers quit doing business with a company is a feeling of indifference they receive from the frontline personnel that serve them. Many times, your customers take personally the type of service they receive. If they receive poor service, it can very easily be interpreted as a form of personal rejection. Conversely, if it is very good service, it can be interpreted as a sign of respect and acceptance. Naturally, our customers prefer the latter form of service.

Taking this discussion one step further, when a person experiences joy or laughter, endorphins are released from the brain. An "endorphin" is a natural morphine-like substance that is produced within the human body. It creates a euphoric-like state that allows a person to experience physical and mental feelings of pleasure. A person feels good. In a similar way, when a person receives the kind of service that can be interpreted as a sign of respect and acceptance, he or she can actually experience a release of endorphins. Thus, when a customer comments to you on how they like doing business with your company, recognize that there is more to it than just words.

What does all of this have to do with your business? The key is to let the fun side of your personality show. Your example will serve as a good role model as well as a reminder for your employees and co-workers. By setting the pace in your business in terms of behavior, your customers, employees and co-workers will appreciate it. The little poem that follows illustrates the point.

By filling your shop with smiles
your customers will come for miles
Ahh, but alas,

if it's a frown upon your face
your customers will shop
some other place
– Tom Borg

1. On a scale of it 1 to 10, 10 being the highest, rate your company or organization on its ability to create a fun environment for both your customers and your employees.

    1 2 3 4 5 6 7 8 9 10
  deadsville   fairville   happyville

2. Name three things you can do or are doing now to make your place of business a fun environment for both your employees and your customers.

a.

b.

c.

3. Hold a meeting and ask for suggestions on how your company or organization can sincerely create a more fun and upbeat atmosphere.

4. Implement one idea per month, for the next three months and re-evaluate the results at the end of the third month.

"An ounce of performance
is worth a ton of excuses."

— Anonymous

TIP #7
BECOME A PROBLEM SOLVER

A number of years ago, I was flying back to Detroit, Michigan on Delta Airlines. After landing in Knoxville to connect with my transfer flight, I checked in at the airline counter and was unpleasantly surprised. At the time I had boarded my originating flight in Dallas, my baggage had been improperly checked to Chicago. Realizing there were only a few minutes before the plane on which I was connecting would be leaving. I anxiously asked the agent if my baggage could possibly be transferred to this flight. He said, "Mr. Borg, (I like being called by name) I'll see what I can do." He then left the counter. He still hadn't returned when the final boarding call for Detroit was given. I reluctantly boarded and sat despondently waiting for the plane to leave without my baggage. Unexpectedly, the pilot announced that our flight would be momentarily delayed while they transferred a passenger's bag to the flight.

The door suddenly opened and onto the airplane walked the agent I had spoken to earlier. He looked around the airplane, saw me sitting in my seat, and came over to me. He knelt down next to me and as I looked at him I could see beads of sweat on his forehead. (I knew he had been up to something!) He said, "Mr. Borg, I want you to know I have personally transferred your bag to this plane. You will be able to pick it up in baggage claim in Detroit. Have a great flight. At the Detroit baggage claim, my bag was the first one to arrive on the conveyor belt. Now that's what I call service! This agent figured out a solution to my dilemma. He was a problem solver.

By becoming a problem solver for our customers, we are communicating to them that we value them as human beings as well as patrons.

ATTITUDE QUIZ:

Answer true or false to the following statements regarding your customers' problems:

1. Whenever a customer expresses a special need, I explain to them that it is not my job.

    True   False

2. If most customers would just take the time to read the signs and the written policies, it would solve half of my headaches.

    True   False

3. I don't have nor want the authority to solve most of my customers' problems.

    True   False

4. Most of my customers are just looking for an opportunity to take advantage of our company policies.

    True   False

5. My main responsibility is getting my work done, not solving my customers' problems.

    True   False

Give yourself 2 points for each false answer and 0 points for each true answer you recorded. If you scored lower than 10 points, your customer service attitude could use some improvement. The answers to this quiz are explained on the next page.

ANSWERS

1. Customers do expect a lot of service. Their special needs are important to them. It's best to resolve needs to the best of your ability.

2. Many times, customers fail to read the signs that have been posted. They expect the employee to have the answers to their questions. They don't want to try and figure out how your system works; they want satisfaction as soon as possible.

3. Customers don't want to know what you CAN'T DO; they want to know what you CAN DO. Do your best to provide the service the customer is looking for.

4. Although it may seem that some of your customers are trying to take advantage of your company, most customers are not. Statistics show that 95-99% of customers are honest. It's important to treat people with trust and respect. Think about how you would like to be treated if you were a customer in someone else's business.

5. Although it may seem that getting your job done is so much more important than dealing with a customer, you wouldn't have a job if there weren't any customers. Make sure you discuss this idea with your staff, co-workers and management and get their suggestions on what is the appropriate action to take when your job responsibilities interfere with serving the customer.

This quiz will give you, your employees and co-workers a good indication of the attitude your company has towards helping your customers solve their problems.

"No man was ever great
by imitation."

— Samuel Johnson

TIP #8
SETTING A NEW PACE FOR CUSTOMER/CLIENT SERVICE – START DOING WHAT YOUR COMPETITION IS TOO LAZY TO DO

I was driving down the main street where I live and noticed a car coming in the opposite direction with four brand new tires. How could I tell they were new? It was easy. I could see the white stickers revolving on the bottom of them as the car came towards me. As the car passed by my vehicle, I could also see that the "white walls" were still colored a pretty blue.

How much longer would it take to remove the white stickers and wash off the blue coloring that covered the white walls? Perhaps only a few extra minutes is all. So, why didn't the tire dealer do it?

It probably just wasn't a priority. Ken Belanger, President of Belanger Tire, a Goodyear tire store in Westland, Michigan, makes it a top priority. He explains that he wants customers "to see what they get." Setting the pace means consistently doing the things that count to the customer.

I walked into a bank one day and was greeted by three consecutive employees. It made me feel good to be acknowledged. As simple as that sounds, those bank employees were setting a new pace for other banks to follow. They were doing something different—making their customers feel important.

Just yesterday, our real estate person, Lee Bittinger of Re-Max Classic, who helped us buy the house my family now lives in, stopped by to say "hi." He commented on how nice our new flower garden looked, and praised me on all the little improvements we had made on the outside of the house. It's been a little over five years since we purchased our home. It seems that he makes it a habit to stop by or to call me at once or twice per year. Is that unusual in the real estate business? You bet it is. This person is a pace setter.

How about your company? Is it doing the best that it can? Is it setting the pace for the competition to follow?

Here are some tips that can help your business move ahead of the competition:

1. Make a list of things that, if done differently, would put the customer's interests first.

2. Make a plan to implement these ideas on a regular basis.

3. Stick to that plan.

As simple as it seems, by following this plan, you will position your business or organization well ahead of the competition.

"Execute every act of life
as though it were thy last."

— Marcus Aurelius

TIP #9
GOING THE EXTRA MILE
FOR YOUR CUSTOMER

It was 4:45 p.m. on a warm Friday afternoon in Traverse City, Michigan. The owner of Ferguson Lawn Supplies and Equipment, Ken Ferguson, and his son Chuck, were just about ready to close for the day. The phone rang and as Chuck answered it, he was greeted by a very desperate voice. It was Bob Jenkins, the general manager of the Grand Hotel on Mackinac Island, one of their customers. The reason for his call to Ferguson Lawn Supplies and Equipment was that they had a very big problem. As Bob Jenkins explained, the Grand Hotel was getting ready for a very prestigious golf tournament that was scheduled to start the next morning. Their one and only Jacobson greens mower, the one that they used to trim the putting green on each hole of the course, had broken down. A few of the spring-loaded spreader fingers that actuated the pressure plate of the clutch assembly had been shattered. The golf course needed to have it repaired immediately, because the greens had to be mowed the next morning at 5:30 a.m.

In the extremely competitive business of lawn supplies and equipment, the Fergusons had a large area to cover. It included the upper half of the state of Michigan and the upper peninsula. Mackinaw City was 110 miles away, not including the ferry boat ride across the straits to the island. In addition to that, no motorized cars or trucks were allowed on the vacation island. It was going to take a minimum of four hours for them to reach the golf course via service truck. Chuck knew they needed to act fast if they were going to help solve this dilemma. After briefly conferring with his dad, Chuck asked Bob Jenkins if he could have the mower loaded onto a horse-drawn wagon and hauled over to the small airport that was located on Mackinac Island. The general manager answered yes, but asked Chuck to explain. Chuck replied that in an emergency like this, the Fergusons could use their family airplane to fly the repairman with the parts necessary to repair the mower. After Chuck hung up the phone, he quickly called down to Larry, his top mechanic, to see if he would be willing to work a little overtime. Larry eagerly agreed. As an extra measure of service, they decided to pull out the back seat of the airplane and load up a brand new Jacobson greens mower to take along as a loaner. Chuck and Larry took off, and when they landed, they were greeted by a very worried Bob Jenkins. Chuck's mechanic, impeccably dressed in his dark blue uniform, shining tool box in hand, went right to work on the disabled mower. It was repaired within 15 minutes. Bob was ecstatic. Then, in a grand gesture, Chuck and his mechanic unloaded the brand new Jacobson greens mower. They explained that they wanted to leave it as a backup (free of charge) just in case anything else went wrong with the repaired mower. They would pick up the loaner on the next service call. The general manager was more than satisfied. The next morning, the greens were mowed and the players commented on how beautiful the golf course looked. The prestigious golf tournament was a success. As it turns out, the brand new Jacobson greens mower never left the island. The general manager thought it would be a good idea to have a back-up mower just in case they ever needed it again.

The story doesn't end there. A few months later, Ken Ferguson and his son attended the Annual Turf Grass Conference at Michigan State University. As they were sitting at their table finishing their dinner, one of their main competitors walked over and said, "Ken, I don't know how you do it. I don't know how you keep the Grand Hotel golf course account. We've been calling on that place for years. We buy that general manager the best steaks, bring him the finest scotch, and we still can't get any of his business! How do you do it?" Ken Ferguson looked up at him and replied "Uhh, I don't know, it sounds like you're doing everything right to me. I wouldn't change a thing." Through this lesson, the message is clear. By going the extra mile for our customers, by being there when they need us, we will keep them as loyal customers for a long, long time.

QUESTIONS FOR EMPLOYEE MEETING:

1. Name one example within the last two months when you went the extra mile for your customer. What could the company have done to make it easier for you to serve the customer?

2. What kinds of things could the company do in the future to prevent these emergencies from happening in the first place?

3. Which company policies are preventing you from going the extra mile for your customer now? Please explain.

4. What kind of positive reinforcement from your staff, co-workers or management would encourage you to satisfy the customer in situations that require you to go the extra mile?

"When you save face for others
your face looks better too.

— Anonymous

TIP #10
DON'T LET YOUR CUSTOMERS LOOK LIKE A BUNCH OF DUMMIES – MAKE IT EASY TO DO BUSINESS WITH YOUR COMPANY

A customer patiently waits in line at the secretary of state's office for license tabs. Finally arriving at the window, he's informed by the clerk that he was in the wrong line and will have to get in line for the next window. The customer feels foolish and deceived. The sign that informs the customers where to stand is not easily seen. The clerk's attitude only adds insult to a bruised ego.

Another customer calls a very busy manufacturing company and is put on hold for two and a half minutes. The switchboard operator finally comes back and connects her with the proper department. If that customer had been given a direct number to dial, she could have saved herself the two and a half minutes she waited, plus a likely toll charge.

Still another customer gets out of her car to pump gasoline at a self-serve station. She inserts the gasoline nozzle into her gas tank receptacle and pulls the trigger. Nothing happens. She stands there befuddled. After looking around for several seconds, a voice blares out over a speaker that she must pay first in order to pump the gas. Startled and embarrassed, she reluctantly heads over to the cashier's window to pay for the privilege of pumping her own gasoline.

Are these stupid customers? No, they are recipients of poor communication. The chances of their satisfaction level being very high are 0 to -3. What could be done to help these customers have a successful experience with the company or organization from which they are trying to receive service?

The management needs to look through the eyes and hear through the ears of the customer. They need to get in touch with what their customers are experiencing. Is the system that is in place making it difficult for the customers to do business with that company or organization? If so, changes are in order.

A simple way to stimulate improvement would be to ask the customer this question: "What are the two most important things we can do to serve you better?"

Once that information is received from a good representation of customers, call a brainstorming session with your entire staff (from management right down to the frontliners). At this session, divide the group so that there are several sub-groups composed of both management and frontline employees. After gathering all the solutions that are generated, implement the best ones. Giving appropriate recognition to those who made the suggestions will enhance future brainstoming sessions. In 30 days, re-evaluate the results by polling your customers and sharing those results with the employees of the company.

In summary, finding out what you can do to make it simpler and easier for your customers to do business with your company, and then doing it, is one important key to increased customer retention.

"To please people is a great step towards persuading them."

— Lord Chesterfield

TIP #11
DON'T TELL YOUR CUSTOMERS — WHAT THEY CAN'T DO —TELL THEM WHAT THEY CAN DO

Have you ever seen these signs posted in various businesses?

If you BREAK IT - you BUY IT.
No Shirt-No Shoes-No Service
We Reserve the Right to Refuse Service to Anyone.
Shoplifters will be prosecuted to the full extent of the law.
CLOSED
Do not lean on the glass display counter.
NO LOITERING

These signs are not very inviting are they? It seems that the owners good intentions have gone astray.

A business associate and I walked into a Mexican-American restaurant for lunch. Our eyes were met by a sign that read, "Banks don't make tacos; we don't accept checks." Next to the words there was a sketch of the owner with a scowl on his face. That first impression had already left a bad taste in my mouth, and we hadn't even sat down to order our meal.

What the owner of this restaurant does not realize is that the message he is sending out to his potential customers is not positive. Actually, it's downright negative. What he's saying is that he doesn't trust his customers.

Is this the message he really wants to express to his customers? Probably not. But, he is expressing it.

A couple of golfing partners decide to try out a new golf course. They walk up to the clubhouse and are met with a barrage of negative signage: "Clean your spikes before entering clubhouse." "Shirt and shoes must be worn at all times." "Replace all divots."

What the owners of this golf course are doing is setting up a negative impression before the first ball is even teed up.

Why do these two examples of poor service in America exist? Because the owners are forgetting a very important truth. Charles Lamb, the great English essayist, said it best when he wrote these words, "Damn it, I like to be liked!" People like to be liked. They don't want to be told what THEY CAN'T DO. They want to be informed of what THEY CAN DO. They want to be made to feel that they are welcome.

A better way for the restaurant owner to inform his clients of the policy of not accepting personal checks could be to tell them what forms of payment he will accept. The sign could read this way:

"Your Visa, Master Charge, Diner's Club, and American Express cards are most welcome. Unfortunately, we do not accept personal checks."

A better way for the golf course to communicate its rules to customers would be to have the signs read this way:

"In order to provide you with a quality golfing experience we ask that all participants follow our rules of golf etiquette. Thanks for your cooperation! As always, it's a pleasure to serve you."

"We want to keep our clubhouse looking it's best for you! Please clean your spikes before entering. Thanks for your cooperation."

"In order to keep our golf course in top condition for everyone's enjoyment, please replace all divots. Thanks for your cooperation!"

"We want you to look your best! Please wear your shirt and shoes on the golf course and in the clubhouse."

The impressions a customer receives when he walks into a business or organization are merely a reflection of the owner's values and people skills and how he or she chooses to express them.

Most restaurants have a sign over the coat rack that reads, "Not responsible for lost or stolen articles." That's what the owner would like you to believe at least. What the sign is really saying is "WE DONT WANT TO BE responsible for lost or stolen articles." Legally, they really are responsible; they just don't want you to know it. Most restaurants that I have surveyed report that they rarely have had anyone lose a coat or a personal belonging. So, my question is why put up the negative sign? Remember, we are trying to make this a positive experience for the customer. Negative signs do not help.

Earl Nightingale used to tell the story of a very popular restaurant in Florida that is still in business today. The customers observe a sign over the coat rack that reads, "Of course we are responsible for your belongings when you are a guest in our restaurant. So, relax, enjoy yourself, and have a good meal. Remember, serving you is our number one purpose." This restaurant has taken a very different approach to reminding its customers that they are important. In so many words, the owner is telling his customers that he cares about them and that he is responsible.

After one of my talks during which I mentioned this restaurant, an elderly woman came up to me and asked, "Where is that restaurant located? My husband and I live down there part of the year and would love to visit it."

How about the sign that appears on most business doors after hours. It usually reads "CLOSED." This sounds so cold and insensitive. It certainly doesn't sound very inviting.

A better idea might be to word it this way: "Unfortunately, our store is now closed: our next opportunity to serve you is 8:30 a.m. We look forward to seeing you."

How can a business avoid giving its customers a negative impression through its signage? First, call a meeting of all employees. Ask the question, "What policies and signs are there in our organization that penalize our customers?" Then take good notes. Ask your customers the same question. Then compare notes. Discuss with your employees how you can change or modify your policies.

How can you re-word negative signs so that they give a positive impression? You may not be able to make everything positive, but the changes you do make will be well-received by your customers. You will begin to set your business apart from the competition and make it a more friendly place to visit.

1. Three signs that you use in your business are:
    a.
    b.
    c.

2. Does each sign get the point across in a positive way?

3. Which signs need to be improved upon? How?

4. Is each sign really necessary? Which ones can you eliminate?

"When people are serving,
life is no longer meaningless."

— John Gardner

TIP #12
VALUE THE LITTLE CUSTOMER; TREAT EACH CUSTOMER AS IF HE OR SHE WAS THE MOST IMPORTANT CUSTOMER

A potential customer called a fence company for an estimate on a split rail fence he wanted installed on residential property. The representative stopped over, gave the client his price, and remarked that it was a minimum size job. The agreement was signed and the salesman promised the work would begin as soon as the homeowner obtained a permit. The homeowner obtained the permit, called the fence company, and left a message for the salesman to notify the work crew to begin as soon as possible. Repeated calls from the potential customer ended in frustration. Obviously, the salesman was very busy, and it was a small job, thus he never bothered to arrange for the work to be done.

A similar situation often happens in the greasy spoon restaurant. The waitress tells two customers just having coffee and discussing their business issues isn't enough to justify serving them. She says they will have to leave because there are too many people waiting in line for a full lunch.

It is pure ignorance on behalf of the owner to allow this type of customer treatment to exist. Borg's Rule:Never ignore a small order—it can cost you big money.

Let's examine the psychology behind that rule. First, even though the job that the customer requested was small, it could be the beginning of a potential relationship that would bring repeat and/or referral business. Second, every customer knows other people. Anytime he is pleased or disappointed about service, he talks to friends and acquaintances. On the average, a customer will tell 5-7 other people of a good experience he has had with a particular business or organization. Good advertising can result from good service. An unhappy customer will tell 9-16 other people of the poor service he has received. Bad advertising usually results from bad service.

How can we avoid offending the customer who has a small order? First and foremost, do your best to give the same kind of service to that customer as you would to a customer with a large order. If that is impossible because your company is just too busy, then I suggest you find one or two smaller businesses to use as referrals for this type of customer. By doing this, you will give the customer the kind of service and respect he deserves.

When it comes to service, far too often the employees of a company or organization make the decision to short-change the customer because they don't see the whole picture.

Remember some people approach their job as if it were a 50 yard dash. They don't realize that they are running a 26 mile 385 yard marathon. Unless the employees change their focus, frustrated customers and lost business will result. Contrary to popular belief, there is not an infinite number of eager customers wanting to buy your product or use your service. In addition to that, there are a growing number of competitors who are vying for those customers.

As a business owner or manager, make it a point to educate your employees on the value of each customer. Make it clear to them that their paycheck depends on long-term satisfied customers. In the long run, your customers, your employees, and your business will benefit.

SELF QUIZ:

Circle the appropriate answers:

1. Our attitude towards a customer with a small order is that:
   a. It's not cost efficient to deal with them.
   b. It prevents us from serving our real customers.
   c. They never come back to buy a bigger order.
   d. They are just a waste of time and energy.
   e. They are an opportunity for us to prove that we mean service.

2. How does our company now deal with a customer who has a small order?
   a. Tell him we are too busy to act on such a small order.
   b. Ignore him and hope he will go away.
   c. Treat him just like a customer who had a big order.
   d. Don't return his phone calls requesting service.
   e. Refer him to a company who will take good care of him.

3. We now use the opportunity to serve a small order customer in the following way:
   a. Let people pass the good word about our commitment to service.
   b. Build a relationship with a customer who may be making a small order now, but has the potential of expanding that order later.
   c. Let the buying public know that we are not designed to deal with the small order customer.

d. Let that customer know that we are far too big and busy to waste time trying to serve the small order customer.

4. Some action steps we could take to improve our rapport with our smaller order customers:
   a. If the order is too small, tactfully refer them to a competent company that will handle the order.
   b. Spend more time and effort working with smaller order customers.
   c. Actively tell and encourage our present customers to let us handle their small orders too.
   d. Stay the same, and keep doing what we've always done.

"You preach a better sermon with your life than with your lips."

— Oliver Goldsmith

TIP #13
GOOD SERVICE STARTS AT THE TOP...SO DOES BAD SERVICE!

Have you ever called the owner or the manager of a company and had them talk to you through their speakerphone? Or have you ever observed how some owners and managers seem to purposely make their next appointment wait for a long time? There are even some who never learned the common rule of etiquette of getting up from behind their desk to greet you.

Bad manners? Absolutely. What's even worse is that it is just plain bad business! Not only does this kind of behavior imply to the customer that this business owner/manager doesn't care, it sets a bad example for the staff and employees.

Customer satisfaction starts at the top. In the above examples, not much will change unless the owners and managers of the company start taking responsibility by modeling basic behavior changes themselves.

It is unfortunate, but true: many business owners and managers are victims of "microwave thinking." They believe that they can quickly "fix" their employees by sending them to a one-day seminar. They think this type of token attempt to train their employees will solve their problems. They fail to see that the overall treatment that their customers receive is the result of an intricately woven set of expectations set up by their own behavior patterns.

An owner's or manager's' gruff treatment of a customer or employee is one of the best ways to teach those same employees the WRONG way to deal with customers. So why do so many owners and managers persist in behaving this way? One reason is that they don't totally realize they are doing it. It's a little like body odor. We all have it. Some of us have a little and some have more, and some are just real "stinkers.

Many times customers and employees are reluctant to tell the arrogant owner or manager that he or she is out of line. The customer would rather shop elsewhere than confront the offensive person, and, of course, for a long time afterwards, they tell as many people as possible about the incompetent idiot who runs or manages the company with whom they PREVIOUSLY did business. In the case of the employee, far too often he or she would rather get along by going along.

Occasionally, the customer will challenge the owner or manager or some brave employee will quit. Of course, the egotistical owner or manager will simply think that the customer is irrational and just hard to please and that the employee is recalcitrant with a personality problem. Many times, the person in charge is a very sensitive individual who has developed a hard-shell personality to serve as a shield against those who disagree with him. I have seen numerous occasions where a "rough tough" owner or manager was verbally attacked by employees, and have then watched as that person reacted like a frightened and immature child. As the old philosophy says, "Pull on the bully's beard and many times you will see that it comes off in your hand."

It seems that there will always be owners and managers of companies who need help in dealing more professionally with their employees and customers. Until those people take responsibility to change their own behavior, they will continue to reap their just and fitting "rewards."

There are some owners and managers who think that if they send their people to a one-day seminar, it will be enough training and education for one year, if not forever. Others think that a six week program will do it. While both of those training experiences are a good place to start, they should not be an end in themselves, but a segment of an overall training and development plan.

1. Rate yourself. On a scale of 1-10, 10 being the highest, how would you rate the example you set for the others in your company or organization?

      1   2   3   4   5   6   7   8   9   10
    poor   so-so   fair   good   excellent

2. When it comes to serving the customer, what is one area you can improve in?

3. How would your company benefit if you were to improve in this area?

4. What action will you take in the next 48 hours to improve in this area?

"Forget your mistakes
but remember
what they taught you."

— Anonymous

TIP #14
HOW TO RECOVER FROM THE MISTAKES YOU MAKE WITH YOUR CUSTOMER

Two customers order breakfast at a nationally known restaurant. The waitress takes their order, thanks them and walks away. A few minutes later, she returns with the two breakfast orders. One of the two customers notices that he didn't get the honey he ordered for his muffins. The waitress comes by a few minutes later, obviously very busy, and checks to see if everything is ok. The customer mentions to her that he didn't get the honey that he ordered. She acknowledges him and promises to get it. Several more minutes go by and nothing happens. Finally, the waitress checks back a second time asking, "Is everything ok?" At this point, the customer explains that it isn't ok. He never did get his honey and eventually just ate his muffins without it. The embarrassed waitress apologizes, murmuring under her breath that they are very busy today. She puts the bill on the table and walks away.

This true story is a good example of good intentions gone astray. The waitress was rushed, and she didn't come through as she had promised her customer. Something as small as the honey for the muffins spoiled the restaurant's opportunity to provide good service to this particular customer. What is remembered in this customer's mind is that this restaurant, not just the waitress, did a lousy job of serving breakfast.

What happened here is not uncommon. Since employees are human, they are going to make mistakes. What is important is how they recover from making the mistakes they've committed.

When a customer receives poor service, he is subconsciously conditioned to expect poor service the next time he does business with that company, that is, unless the company does something that would offset the experience in a positive way.

In the example we talked about earlier, the waitress could have deducted the muffins from the cost of the breakfast and she could have given the customer a certificate for a free breakfast the next time he returned.

The main point here is to let the customer know that you value him or her as someone important and that satisfaction with your product or service is crucial. You might make mistakes, but you're going to correct those mistakes and offer compensation.

An important point to note when you are making up for the mistake is to have a "bring back factor" built in. This means that whatever you do to correct the error committed, make sure that it is something that will bring the customer back to your place of business. This will give you an opportunity to replace the negative expectation of service with a positive expectation. In the restaurant example above, the certificate for a future free breakfast would give the restaurant another chance to prove to the customer that it can provide excellent service.

1. What are some particular situations in your business where a customer could experience poor service or an inferior product?

2. What kinds of things could your company do to make up for a faulty product or an error in service?

3. What kind of a "bring back factor" could you build into it?

4. What steps could you, your staff, co-workers and managers take to prevent these things from happening?

"The only limits
are, as always,
those of vision."

— James Broughton

TIP #15
DO THE UNEXPECTED

One summer, Elizabeth, my wife and I took a vacation through Northern Michigan. On a particular day we had several places we wanted to visit so we started out very early from the town of St Ignace. To save time, we decided we would stop for breakfast a few hours later. However, my wife just had to have a cup of gourmet coffee before we got on the road. Problem, all the gourmet coffee shops were not open yet. We searched around and finally spotted a place that served gourmet coffee called the Colonial Lodging Bed and Breakfast. It didn't look quite open yet, however, Elizabeth decided she would take a chance and find out if they would serve her.

Upon entering the bed and breakfast she discovered a most delightful man, who just happened to be the owner. He explained to her that they were not quite open yet, but he had just finished brewing up some of their special gourmet coffee and poured her a cup. Elizabeth asked him how much she owed him and he replied "no charge, have a great day!"

What the owner of the Colonial Lodging Bed and Breakfast did that day for my wife was unexpected. He left an extremely positive feeling with her. He did something that can only build good will and in the long term his business.

Are there a lot of bed and breakfast establishments out there? Yes, and as we all know it can be very competitive in that market just like it is in your market place. So why not do something positive for your potential as well as your existing customers – do the unexpected.

Some of the things to consider that fall under this category include.

• Opening and closing your store a few minutes earlier than the posted sign indicates.

• Providing the extra few cents for a customer's purchase so he or she doesn't have to break a dollar.

• Acknowledge them as soon as they walk in the door with a cheery hello and "we will be right with you".

• Make them feel truly welcome. Let them know you really care about meeting their needs and wants.

• If they couldn't find what they wanted in your store recommend them to a place where they can find it.

• Ask them was everything alright with their purchase and mean it. If something was not, do your best to make it right.

1. Start taking notes on the kind of things other businesses do that are "unexpected ". Ask your self how that could be incorporated into your business.

2. At your next staff meeting challenge the group to come up with a list of things they could do that would be a pleasant surprise to the customer. Decide as a company which ones would be practical to implement. Positively reinforce your employees and co-workers when they do what is "unexpected" for the customer.

3. In the space below compile a list of things you could possibly do that would fall under the category of "The Unexpected".

"The greatest deception
men suffer is
from their own opinions."

— Leonardo da Vinci

TIP #16
PROVIDE A SUGGESTION
BOX FOR THE CUSTOMER

The Canton Public Library in Canton, Michigan has an outstanding reputation for service. It is ranked as one the top libraries in the state for the type of services it provides as well as its high number of patrons.

This library has everything from a receptionist who greets each person to a large reading room with a fireplace. What also adds to the atmosphere is a piano-shaped window section with a natural view that provides a great place to curl up with a book. A very supportive library board and a top-notch library director, Jean Tabor, help make this library customer-oriented. The director was wise enough to tap the creative potential of her employees in designing the new library. In addition to that, several surveys were conducted before the new library was built to find out what the public wanted. The results have been a library that has pleased both the staff and the patrons. The library is open 7 days per week and is always busy.

One of the main reasons this library is so successful is because of its willingness to find out what the patrons want. People using the library are encouraged to make suggestions that will help make it a better place. A suggestion box is in plain sight, complete with paper and pencils. The steady flow of suggestions received weekly are reviewed and promptly acted upon. Each person who makes a suggestion is contacted and thanked. This suggestion box system works very effectively for the Canton Public Library.

The management of many organizations and companies complain that they've tried using suggestion boxes and they just don't work. They probably don't work because they are not properly administered. In order for a customer's suggestion box to be effective, management must treat it as an important tool that can improve the organization.

The important thing to remember is to make sure that all suggestions are responded to and the best ones implemented.

If you now have a suggestion box for your customers, consider how you can improve its effectiveness by answering the following questions:

1. Is it in the best location for your customers to see and use?

2. How could you and your staff and co-workers actively encourage your customers to make suggestions?

3. What kind of an incentive can your company give to your customers for making suggestions?

4. How does your company now respond to each customer making a suggestion?
   a. Written thank you
   b. Telephone call
   c. Verbal communication
   d. Ignore the person completely

5. If you don't have a suggestion box, when will you get one?

"You can dream, create, design and build the most wonderful place in the world . . . but it takes people to make the dream a reality."

— Walt Disney

TIP #17
HIRE THE BEST PEOPLE

One of the best ways to put a smile on your employee or manager's face is to make sure there is one already there before you hire that person. When you seek to hire an employee or a manager, make sure you are hiring a person who understands that the customer is really the one who signs his or her paycheck. Seek out people who have a good attitude and truly like themselves. In today's market, it is getting more and more competitive to find and hire well-qualified people. Don't let that deter you. Look for employees and managers with potential, and give them a chance to learn how to perform at their job.

There are some excellent measuring instruments on the market today that can help you evaluate behavior tendencies of the job applicants you are considering for employment. By no means should these tools be the only method by which you screen job applicants. However, they can be an excellent guide in helping you make the final selection. Contact my office for the name and telephone numbers of some of these companies.

Regardless of who you hire, you must develop the knack of recognizing latent talents in that person. Be willing to work with the employee. Some are quick learners; others are slower. It seems that the ones who take longer to learn basic skills remain with your company longer than others who may grow bored and restless and look for greener pastures. The key is to be patient when helping your new employees develop the necessary skills required to perform their job. By giving them a chance to develop into good employees, (some of these employees will eventually become good managers) you will build the reputation of your company so much that it can be a reason for other potential employees to be attracted to it.

Hire the Best People

1. How do you now determine what qualities are important for a new employee position?

2. Ask your employees what qualities are necessary to do their jobs properly.

3. What criteria do you use to decide if new hires are kept as permanent employees?

4. How do you reward good employees for their longevity with your company?

"It is not what he has,
nor even what he does,
which directly expresses
the worth of a man,
but what he is."

— Henri Frederic Amiel

TIP #18
LOOK 'EM SQUARE IN THE EYE AND SINCERELY SAY "THANK YOU"

One way for a company to set itself apart from the rest of the competition at the point of sale would be to teach its' employees to look the customer squarely in the eye and sincerely thank them for doing business with them.

There is a very well-known retail chain that has even printed by the cash register what it wants the cashier to say to the customer when the sale is completed. At one time, this retail chain even had a campaign giving the customer five dollars if the cashier didn't say "thank you." Unfortunately, it didn't work. The result was a cashier who sounded like a robot and avoided making sincere eye contact with the customer at the close of the sale.

What the management of this retail chain did not understand was that it was not possible to force its cashiers to be sincerely courteous to the customer.

Since you can't force your staff, co-workers and managers to treat the customer courteously in person or on the phone, how do you work toward getting that kind of consistent behavior from your them? One way to make this hope a reality is to hire people who have three important qualities:

1. They like themselves.
2. They like other people.
3. They have a sincere desire to help and serve other people.

First, you have to hire people having some realization of the above qualities. From there you educate, train, and reinforce them for consistently demonstrating sincere courtesy in action.

What we are talking about is helping staff, co-workers and management learn how to be more authentic, helping them develop their self-confidence to the level where it is easy for them to treat others with courtesy and respect. The example you set is the most important aspect. How you treat your staff, co-employees and managers lays the groundwork for how they will treat the customer.

1. What types of traits do you look for in the staff and managers you seek to hire?

2. What are two things you, your staff, co-workers and managers can do for each other to set the pace on how to treat the customer?

3. Name two specific things that you, your staff, co-workers and managers can do to demonstrate their respect for the customer?

"Training is everything.
The peach was once a bitter
almond; cauliflower is nothing
but a cabbage without
a college education."

— Mark Twain

TIP #19
MAKE SURE YOUR EMPLOYEES KNOW HOW THEY ARE EXPECTED TO PERFORM

Do your employees understand how they are expected to perform? How do you, as a business owner or manager, know? Many times, the reason for employees not performing properly is because they do not fully understand their responsibilities. They don't know what they can do and what they can't do. Often, an employee will find out what he or she is not supposed to do only after it's done.

The reason the employee didn't know is because the company or organization failed to inform him or her. Improperly reprimanding employees for something that was not properly explained to them can be a real de-motivator.

One way to prevent this predicament from occurring is to have a structured orientation for all new employees. Explain to them that the only dumb question is the one that is not asked. Your job is to make sure that they understand and are able to meet their job requirements.

That leads us to the next question. Are your employees able to perform as expected? Even though employees understand what they are supposed to do doesn't mean they can perform at an acceptable level. A greeter at a restaurant needs to be a people-oriented person, able to interact effectively with the customers who come through the door. Even though job responsibilities are understood, if that person acts shy and introverted, it's likely that he or she will fail miserably in that particular position. If you have an employee who is expected to do inventory and he or she has trouble doing basic math, you could be in for a disappointing job performance. Screen your applicants carefully.

Make Sure Your Employees Know How to Perform

1. Do you provide an orientation session for all new employees?

2. Ask your present employees for suggestions on how to improve it.

3. Make a list of performance requirements for each job. Make sure your employees understand them.

4. Stress the importance of being able to perform as expected.

"If you think education is expensive
— try ignorance."

— Derek Bok
President, Harvard University

TIP #20
PROVIDE CUSTOMER SERVICE TRAINING AND EDUCATION FOR YOUR EMPLOYEES

Could you imagine a collision shop hiring a person with no prior experience for the job of repairing damaged cars or a company hiring someone to work as a computer operator with no knowledge or skill in using a computer? It wouldn't make sense to hire someone for a position like that unless that person received the necessary training to perform satisfactorily at that job.

Yet, employees are hired everyday to fill positions that put them face to face with the customer. They receive little or no training and education in dealing with customers, yet are expected to perform effectively. Many businesses don't recognize the importance of hiring qualified people and making sure they receive the training and education necessary to be successful at serving the customer.

Often, a business or organization assumes that the employees they hire have the necessary skills to deal with people. They may have some of the skills, but rarely do they have all of the competence necessary to do the job right.

Survey after survey has shown that the number one reason customers switch the store or company where they do business is due to a feeling of indifference shown them by the employee serving them.

Employees come into contact with customers in several different ways. The cashier, stock person, manager, and person who answers the telephone all serve a vital link in satisfying that customer. By not being given the necessary tools to deal effectively with their customers, employees and managers do what comes naturally. Unfortunately, many times that can be the wrong thing.

Companies unwilling to spend time and money to train and educate their employees properly usually find their turnover high and customer satisfaction low. These kinds of businesses can and do survive if the business climate is in their favor. However, once there is a downswing in the economy or a competitor moves into the area who is committed to providing real service to the customer, watch out. Drastic changes in the bottom line of the shoddy service provider will follow.

A nationally known print shop had been in business in a mid-size town for several years.

Since the area was large enough to support two printing facilities, another franchise was sold to a different person across town. The new franchise owner hired the right people, provided the necessary training for her employees, and started providing quick, courteous, and accurate service to her customers. It wasn't long before she was dominating that market.

It is a bit odd, but remember that the average American company spends 5-6 times more money to attract new customers through advertising and promotions than it does to keep the ones it already has. Yet, time and time again, the companies that spend money to properly train and educate their employees get better results.

Elizabeth Duke, president of the Bank of Tidewater in Virginia Beach, Virginia, believes her bank is successful because of the way her employees treat the customer. She says, "My employees are specially trained to concentrate on what the customer needs. - Duke spends no money on costly advertising campaigns; she just concentrates on having her employees treat the customer the way the customer would like to be treated. Despite the fact that the bank has spent no money on advertising since its opening in 1985, 35% of its new customers have come to her as the result of referrals from her satisfied customer base.

Most businesses would never dare to cut out all advertising through the media, but more and more businesses are taking a portion of that advertising dollar and creating a training budget for their employees. The key is to provide the best on-going training and education programs possible for your employees. The results will be worth it.

1. How much do you spend on advertising per year?

2. What kind of budget do you have for the ongoing training and education of your employees?

3. How much does the turnover of an employee cost your company in dollars and cents?
   a. $500 or less
   b. $500-$1,000
   c. $1,000-$1,500
   d. $1,500 or more
   e. Don't know

4. How much training do new employees receive?
   a. One week or more of classroom and on-the-job training and quarterly training on a periodic basis
   b. One day or more of classroom and on-the-job training
   c. One half day of classroom and on-the-job training
   d. One hour or less of classroom and on-the-job training
   e. We don't really have a training program for training new employees.

5. How does your training of employees compare to your competition's approach?

"When people talk,
listen completely.
Most people never listen."

— Ernest Hemingway

TIP #21
HOLD REGULAR MEETINGS TO KEEP COMMUNICATION LINES OPEN

Good public relations begins at home. Happy staff equals happy customers. Meaningful and regular staff meetings can be a very powerful tool in helping your company meet the needs and expectations of your customers. As situations come up, mini-meetings and brain-storming sessions that quickly solve problems can also be used very effectively.

Regular meetings held with a purpose can keep the lines of communication open.

Often employees feel stymied in their ability to communicate their feelings and viewpoints to management. The staff feel like second-rate people because they are never given an opportunity to be heard. What most organizations lack is a structure to insure that the meetings are held on a regular basis.

To insure that the meetings are effective, it is important that some preparation be made before each meeting. What are the challenges that need to be addressed? What is being done about the issues that were discussed at the last meeting? What is going right? Why? How can we make things even better? By asking these kinds of questions, you are building a framework to give communication within your company a place to grow and develop.

By holding meaningful and action-oriented meetings, you make it easy for your employees to communicate with each other as well as with management. Many times, it's not a "generation gap" that prevents teamwork within a company, but a "communication gap." By following through with a plan for communicating, you are insuring a clearer, more effective form of constant communication in your company. As a result, by keeping miscommunication to a minimum, you will have a happier and more productive group of employees.

1. How often do you hold meetings with your employees?
    a. Once per week,
    b. Once per month,
    c. Once per year (whether we need it or not).
    d. Don't have time for them.

2. Do you have a written agenda to follow?

3. Do your employees have a copy of that agenda?

4. Is it distributed at least 24 hours before the meeting?

5. Is there action taken to insure that miscommunications and problems are corrected?

6. Name a few topics and problems you need to address at your next meeting?

7. How do you encourage your employees to ask questions —even "dumb" questions?

8. How do you make sure the main points of the meeting are summarized?

"If you would lift me
you must be on higher ground."

— Ralph Waldo Emerson

TIP #22
TAKE A SINCERE INTEREST IN EACH ONE OF YOUR EMPLOYEES

Many employers pay their employees a fair monetary wage. However, when it comes to taking a sincere interest in them as human beings, these same employers fail. It is no secret today that many young people come from broken homes. They often lack the guidance that comes from a parent who is willing to patiently listen and understand that young adult. Yes, they have their unique ways of dressing and behaving, but so did you when you were growing up.

What an employer can do to create a more satisfied staff is to develop an attitude of treating his or her employees as human beings with a need to feel important. It's been said that if you talk to people about themselves, they will listen to you for hours. People want to feel important. By taking a sincere interest in them, you are communicating that they are somebody special. You will learn a few things you probably wouldn't know otherwise, while building the self-esteem of your employees. People don't care how much you know, but they do know how much you care. Remember, each one of your employees is truly a special person and is unique in his or her own way.

1. Write out a list of the names of your employees.

2. Make time to talk to each one of them. Find out some of the things they consider important in their lives.

3. Take notes and make it a point to discuss these things with them from time to time.

"A man can succeed at almost anything for which he has unlimited enthusiasm."

— Charles Schwab

TIP #23
PROVIDE THE RIGHT INCENTIVES FOR YOUR EMPLOYEES TO DO THEIR JOB WELL

Some of your employees, although they know what is expected of them and how to perform, simply do not do it consistently. A vivid example of the above is the typical behavior of cashiers in self-service gas stations. These employees sit behind a bullet-proof window and think that their job is to simply take the customer's money. They often do this while simultaneously talking on the phone, chewing gum, or chatting with a fellow employee. That type of behavior is definitely not service-oriented.

The question that must be asked is: Are there valued rewards for performing as expected? Just because employees understand and are able to perform as expected doesn't mean they will. Your employees need to be continually reinforced for doing things right. The attitude of some business owners and managers is, "They collect a paycheck; that's all the positive reinforcement they need." That type of thinking is not only short-sighted, it's pure ignorance. Your employees need to consistently receive rewards they value.

While it's true that you can't really motivate your employees - they have to motivate themselves - there are some things you can do as an owner or manager to create the proper environment for employees to provide their own self-motivation, i.e., to do what is expected of them. To do this, you need to find out what motivates your employees.

In a survey conducted by a national business magazine it was revealed, once again, that money was not the top motivator for most people between the ages of 16 and 40 years. What the survey found was that aspects like gratifying work, appreciation for a job well done, recognition, and a feeling of independence in the way they performed their job responsibilities were at the top of the list. Money ranked in the middle.

So, how do you find out what specifically motivates your employees? Ask them. Remember, the number one stumbling block to knowing what your employees are thinking and feeling is not the generation gap but the communication gap. Sit down with each of your employees and ask them what they like about their jobs. Find out how they feel about interacting with their cus-

tomers and how they like to be shown appreciation for a job well done.

Keep in mind that, depending on their viewpoint and life situation, their answers may vary.
One month it may be recognition; another
month it may be money. Also inquire how they
want to be treated when they make a mistake.
Once you find out what some of their self-moti-
vators are, make it a point to use them. By doing
so, you will be on your way to creating a more
customer-oriented team.

SUGGESTED ACTION:

Set up a personal meeting with each one of your employees and ask the following questions:

1. What do you like about your job?

2. What do you dislike about your job?

3. What do you like most about dealing with your customers?

4. What do you like least about dealing with your customers?

5. How do you like to be shown appreciation for a job well done?

6. How do you want to be treated when you make a mistake?

"Climb High
Climb Far
Your Goal the Sky
Your Aim the Star."
— Inscription on Hopkins Memorial Steps
Williams College, Williams town,
Massachusetts

TIP #24
KEEP YOUR EMPLOYEES ON A GROWTH CURVE

How many times have you walked into a store and had to put up with a bored clerk who waited on you? The clerk had probably grown tired of his job. Perhaps he had reached the point where his duties were no longer a challenge. This scenario is a common one. It plagues businesses and organizations all over the nation.

Surveys suggest that as high as 60%-80% of the people employed in America do not like their jobs. Not only is that a waste of human potential, it creates lousy service for the customer. It is extremely important to match the right employee to the right position. Certainly it helps to have your employees work as many different positions as possible. The Japanese call it cross training. It helps to keep your employees excited about the part they play in providing the kind of service your customers need and want. By giving your employees the chance to work different jobs, you are providing them with the opportunity to learn and grow. Word will get around that your business is the place to seek employment, because you are helping people build their careers.

Some business owners argue that it's easier to have the same employee do the same job, day in and day out, because it keeps the quality more consistent. The truth of the matter is that the average employee, with the right training, is capable of adequately performing several different types of jobs. When the time comes that you can no longer challenge that person with the type of jobs available to them at your company, encourage them to move on. It's not fair to your employee or your business to prevent them from growing. Remember the saying, "When you are green you grow, and when you are ripe you rot."

Suggestions for keeping your employees on a growth curve:

1. Create a flow chart of the different skills and responsibilities your employees can learn and master in your company.

2. Explain to them how these skills can be a valuable tool in the long-term development of their careers, whether with your company or any other.

3. Ask your employees what kinds of things they want to learn.

4. Ask your employees for suggestions on how you can make their job more challenging and rewarding.

"The best executive is the one who has sense enough to pick good men to do what he wants done, and self-restraint enough to keep from meddling with them while they do it."

— Theodore Roosevelt

TIP #25
DELEGATE ADDITIONAL RESPONSIBILITY

Have you ever considered the idea of letting your employees take charge of doing a job the way the way they think it should be done? Let them put their creative talents to work. Most people use only a fraction of their potential brain power. Why not give your employees a chance to use more of theirs?

Avoid the philosophy, "We've done it this way for years, so why change a good thing?" That's "dead end" thinking and often leads to frustration and complacency. With a reasonable amount of structure, your employees should be able to use their creative talents quite well. Of course, you will have to be somewhat flexible, and from time to time live with a few mistakes, but the increased productivity can be worth it. The key here is good communication. Ask your employees to share the idea with you before they try using it. Ask your other employees what they think of the idea. If it sounds like it has some real potential, try it.

What if we had stubbornly resisted Thomas Edison and his idea of the electric light bulb? Why, we would all be sitting around watching television in the dark! All kidding aside, many times our employees will figure out a better way to do the job than it has been done in the past.

Giving your employees the freedom to do the job as they think it should be done communicates your trust in them. People in general like to be trusted. It bolsters their self-confidence. Trusting and believing in your employees allows them to believe in themselves. Remember, when you concentrate on building your people, you will build your business.

1. In which jobs can you allow your employees to use their creative talents?

2. How could your customers benefit by your employees' ability to creatively handle their jobs?

"Too many men who know all about financial values know nothing about human values."

— Roy L. Smith

TIP #26
GIVE ALL YOUR EMPLOYEES THEIR OWN BUSINESS CARD   -IT'S IMPORTANT TO MAKE THEM FEEL IMPORTANT

There is a vice-president of a general contracting company who believes in his employees. He believes in them to the point where he has purchased business cards (not the kind that they have to write their name on) for all of them. It doesn't matter if the person's a truck driver or a bulldozer operator. When he was questioned about this "needless expenditure" by another officer in the company, the vice-president explained that since each of his employees was representing the company, he believed that they needed and merited having a business card. The vice-president knew that each person in his company wanted and deserved to feel important, and that a paycheck wasn't the only thing that kept them working for the company.

The simple use of a business card is just one example of how we can help make all of our employees feel more important. When we give them the psychological income they deserve, the chances of their being more caring and concerned about their customers will increase.

Have you ever stopped to think that your employees are one of your most important forms of advertising? How your employees are perceived by the customer can have a major impact on whether or not that customer will return.

ACTION PLAN:

Make a list of all of the employees in your company who do not have a business card. Be sure to include all of your employees: secretaries, receptionists, shipping clerks, bookkeepers, etc. Include them all.

Call a company meeting and explain that everyone of them plays an important part in making the company successful. Point out that when they are on or off the job they represent the company, and they all have a role in helping the company to serve the clients and customers. Explain just how important it is that they all have a business card. Find out how each person (who does not already have a business card) wants his or her name and position printed on that card.

If possible, when the cards come back from the printer, personally deliver the business cards to the employees. Again, reinforce how much you value them as part of the company. By doing so, you will help build their feelings of importance and allegiance to your company, on and off the job.

"Correction does much,
but encouragement does more."

— Goethe

TIP #27
IMPLEMENT A SYSTEM THAT REGULARLY RECOGNIZES AND REWARDS YOUR EMPLOYEE'S OUTSTANDING JOB PERFORMANCE

One of the best ways to get the kind of behavior you want is to outline specific criteria for identifying outstanding job performance. Then consistently reward it when you get it. By putting together an incentive program for your employees, you are making a positive statement that you value good work.

Find out the kinds of incentives and rewards that are important to your employees and managers by asking them. You can do this in one-on-one conversations or in staff meeting. Once the program is instituted, be sure to constantly work at improving it. If the program is started and there is no follow-through, it can result in creating cynicism and resentment.

The awards don't have to be fancy cars or elaborate trips to Hawaii. Something quite simple and inexpensive will work. It could be a dinner for two at a popular restaurant. A gift certificate to a popular retail store or a picture of the employee or manager in the monthly newsletter or on the wall in the lobby is also effective. Other ideas include a special designated parking spot for a month or a framed certificate of achievement. All awards should include a personal word of thanks from the president or owner.

The key to an effective award system is that it should be ongoing and include something that will be remembered. Sometimes, although a cash reward is appropriate, many employees and managers will end up spending the money on bills. The result? They don't remember anything special from earning the award.

Once you've decided on the approach you will take, call a general meeting with all of your employees and managers. At this time, explain to them why you are instituting the incentive program and explain how it will work. Make sure they understand the process. By encouraging questions and suggestions, you will help employees feel more comfortable with it. After one month, make any necessary adjustments. Re-evaluate it on a regular basis and constantly work on improving and refining it.

One special note here about the awards that are given out: make the person receiving the award feel special. People like to receive the recognition due to them; they like to feel important. I remember one manager telling me that he once had worked for a different company, and was to receive a special award at the annual banquet. He finished his shift earlier that evening and hurriedly drove over to the hotel where the banquet was being held. By the time he arrived, the awards ceremony was nearing completion. The president had already passed his name earlier, and thus ignored his presence because he did not want to slow the evening agenda. This employee felt invalidated and hurt. Don't make a similar mistake with your awards system.

By using a system to consistently reward your employees and manager, you will create a built-in incentive system for them to constantly strive to do the best job possible.

1. What type of an incentive system could you implement in your company?

2. What kind of efforts would you reward?

3. How much could you budget for this system?

4. What kind of incentives or rewards would you be able to provide to your outstanding employees?

"Whoever admits he is too busy
to improve his methods
has acknowledged himself to be
at the end of his rope."

— J. Ogden Armour

TIP #28
USE AN EMPLOYEE SUGGESTION BOX

One excellent way that will help keep your employees motivated and help gather great ideas on improving your business is to use an employees' suggestion box. It's no surprise that many of the answers to the customer service problems you face in your business can come from your employees. In many of the businesses that we surveyed that had a suggestion box, the biggest response showed it was seldom used. It's probable that the suggestion box was not given enough support by management, resulting in an attitude of "Why bother?"

One company reported outstanding success with their suggestion box. This organization used a "Quality Service Committee" approach. The way it worked was that a representative took the suggestions to the committee each month. The person who made the suggestion remained anonymous. Each suggestion made was given careful consideration by the committee. If it was a good one, it was implemented.

The important thing to remember is to make sure that all employee suggestions are responded to and the best ones implemented. In some companies, rewards are given to the people who made the suggestions that are used. The reward could be something quite simple, such as mentioning their name at the next meeting and giving them a certificate of appreciation or perhaps a gift certificate to a local restaurant or a popular retail store. It's important to let them know you appreciate their willingness to offer their suggestions.

It's a real de-motivator for any employee to have a carefully constructed suggestion ignored by management. Remember, if all suggestions are acknowledged, it will positively reinforce the idea of giving suggestions. One note of caution: never openly criticize any suggestion offered. That type of action will only discourage others from contributing their ideas. In one organization, the newly instituted suggestion box was opened at the monthly employees' meeting. The manager went through the suggestions and read them aloud. He openly criticized the ones he didn't like, often making the comment, "Hmmmph! That will never work." Curiously, after that meeting, the employees never bothered to use the suggestion box again.

1. Does your company now use an employee suggestion box?

2. Where would be a good place to put it?

3. When would be the best time to review the suggestions?

4. What kind of rewards would you give to the employees who suggest the ideas that are used?

5. How would you acknowledge the employee who made suggestions that were not used?

"The people who get on in this world are the people who get up and look for the circumstances they want, and if they can't find them make them."

— George Bernard Shaw

TIP #29
MARKET YOUR COMPANY'S SERVICES TO THE MAJOR ETHNIC GROUPS IN YOUR AREA

Drakeshire Dental Center in Farmington, Michigan is doing something unique. It is making a concerted effort to market its dental services to the Japanese population. One of the three partners, Karson Carpenter, DDS, explained that once they identified the fact that there was a strong concentration of Japanese people located within a ten mile radius of their office, they knew they had a unique opportunity. They capitalized on that opportunity by catering to that particular ethnic group. Business cards and signs at the reception desk are printed in Japanese. Even the restrooms have both Japanese and American signage on them. Dr. Carpenter says that it is no accident that his clinic has established a positive reputation with the Japanese-Americans. Their

Japanese clientele is now 5% of their total patient base and growing.

America is known for its highly mixed culture base. The ethnic pipeline within the different ethnic groups can be a very powerful marketing tool. If your company or organization does an outstanding job of servicing its customers, word will get around. If it goes a step further in meeting the needs of certain ethnic groups, word will get around even quicker. How do you find out what a certain ethnic group prefers in the way of your product or service? Simple. Ask the ethnic customers you now have. Ask them what they like the most about doing business with you. If there was one thing your organization could do to serve them better, what would it be? What would it mean to them if you could give them that kind of special service?

Just because a person from another country has decided to move to the United States doesn't mean that they have forgotten their homeland.

Think for a moment about your own childhood. Were there some unique characteristics about your old neighborhood that you really enjoyed? Maybe it was that quaint neighborhood grocery store. If some of those characteristics were present in a grocery store today, you would probably enjoy shopping there. You probably wouldn't mind driving the extra miles to get there. You'd just feel more comfortable doing business at that type of store.

Remember, we human beings are creatures of habit. We prefer the familiar and the predictable. By becoming aware of your potential ethnic market, you may open up an opportunity to serve your real customer base.

1. What ethnic groups are predominant in your business area?

2. How can you find out? (Your local chamber of commerce is one good place to start.)

3. What are some questions you can ask the members of those ethnic groups that will help you identify their unique needs and wants?

4. Set up a "get acquainted" meeting with a few people from that ethnic group. Ask them how your business could better serve their ethnic group.

5. Get together with some other local business owners and brainstorm how you could service this particular ethnic group.

6. What other kinds of things can you do to let a particular ethnic group in your area know that you have its different preferences in mind?

"We can be valued only
as we make ourselves valuable."

— Emerson

TIP #30
WHAT ABOUT SERVICE CONTRACTS?

Have you noticed the many companies selling service contracts for their products or service? Some of the companies using service contracts are automobile dealerships, appliance stores, heating and cooling contractors. These are just a few of the companies that offer service contracts. There are many more.

There are two schools of thought on service contracts. The first is that it gives the customer the opportunity to buy added protection against potential defects in the product or service that the company is selling.

The second school of thought is that service contracts are not necessary. They are simply an excuse for sloppy workmanship, and at the same time very profitable for the company selling them. The one who loses is the customer.

Ron Zemke, one of the most respected individuals in the field of customer service training and development, believes that the future will bring a trend for people to buy only products which are unconditionally guaranteed. Consumers will be unwilling to tolerate the service contract mentality.

It's my opinion that companies should unconditionally stand behind the products and services that they sell. They should not try to charge the customer more for a so-called 'service contract." Yes, from time to time a product will fail or service will not be up to the proper standards. However, rather than charging the customer more money with a service contract, why not just give them what they paid for in the first place? The companies and organizations that will be most successful will be the ones that set the pace in this area. People want quality and service that they can depend on--without having to pay for a service contract.

Can you imagine a scenario of medical doctors selling service contracts? Think about it. Let's say they were going to do a heart transplant. For an additional $5000, they would guarantee the heart for two full years! Apply this strategy to restaurants. For an extra $5 they would guarantee clean tableware, fish grilled to perfection, and, of course, a very courteous waitress or waiter. Switch now to hair stylists. For an extra $20, they would guarantee a punctual appointment with a cut and style done the way you like it. Who knows, for an extra $5 they might not even smoke cigarettes just before your appointment with them, and might even display some current magazines in the waiting area.

Yes, I know I'm stretching things a bit with the suggestion of service contracts for doctors, waitresses, and hair stylists. It wouldn't be practical. Why? Because we expect that they are providing the best service possible to begin with, although many of them don't and we simply put up with it or take our business elsewhere. The point I'd like to make is that most businesses (including new car dealers) should guarantee great service and full satisfaction without customers having to buy a service contract.

Service contracts simply don't make sense for the consumer. The company that implements a strategy guaranteeing unconditional quality and service at no extra charge will demonstrate to its competitors that this approach can be a key factor in keeping customers loyal indefinitely and the operation profitable and successful.

1. Does your company sell service contracts?

2. Does the competition sell service contracts?

3. How could you position your company in the market place by guaranteeing all of the products and services your company sells - without a service contract?

4. If you can't unconditionally guarantee all of your products and services, which ones could you guarantee?

EPILOGUE

Well, here are 30 tips for helping you win big in small business. Like all suggestions, you should take them one at a time and try them out. Re-evaluate them after 30 days or six months. Look for signs of improvement in the attitude of your employees and your customers, as well as yourself. Keep using the ones that work well in your situation.

Remember, things change slowly. It may take awhile. But, like a master gardener, if you continue to nurture and care for the tiny flower seed that has been planted, it will develop a solid root system. It will grow and flourish. It is the same for the service strategy you are growing with your small business. As the owner, manager or employee, you can be the master gardener. Through patience and persistence, your business, too, will flourish.

Just one person with a clear idea of what he or she wants, along with a driving desire to make it happen — can make it happen. That single person, with the help of his or her team, can create the type of customer-oriented business that turns heads when people drive by. It starts with a desire and a willingness to follow through. If you have read this book to its conclusion, I believe you have what it takes to follow through. The time to start is now! I wish you the very best of success!

AFTERWORD

Now that you have read this book, you can understand why Tom Borg is one of the brightest new stars in customer service training, consulting and motivation.

Here is a book that blends real motivation and inspiration with highly workable nuts and bolts. Tom is a person whose concept of service is fully in consonance with the following quotes and statements:

—Gandhi said, "You will find yourself by losing yourself in service to your fellow man, your country and your God."

—Holy Scripture says: "He who would be the master must first be the servant of all."

—The words "sell" and "serve" came from the same root word. Their meaning is identical.

Read this book again and again. It will enable you to enrich the lives of others by the richness of your own.

Joe Batten
Author of the
"Tough-Minded" Books

ORDER FORM

Please send me:

Copies

_____ Making Service Count – How to Deliver Outstanding Customer Service and Make Your Small Business More Profitable

@$14.95 per book $_____

Tom's other book:

_____ Natural Prescriptions for the Good Life –

@$12.95 per book $_____

Total: $ _____

Michigan residents add 6% sales tax $ _____

For shipping and handling add $4.95 per book $ _____

Grand Total $ _____

Your Name: _____

Address:_____

City: _____State: _____ Zip _____

Phone Number: (_____)_____

Photo copy, FAX or return this page to:

Tom Borg

6426 Kings Mill Ct.

Canton, MI 48187

FAX (734) 453-8415

For multiple or bulk order pricing call (734) 453-8019

Thank you for your order!